Georgian Dream

"Every journey has its own secret purpose, of which the traveler himself has no idea."

- Martin Buber -

Georgian Dream

Ilya Tsarev

Published by BoyJah Publishing LLC, 2024.

While every precaution has been taken in the preparation of this book, the publisher assumes no responsibility for errors or omissions, or for damages resulting from the use of the information contained herein.

GEORGIAN DREAM

First edition. April 23, 2024.

ISBN: 979-8224973606

Written by Ilya Tsarev.

Also by Ilya Tsarev

Sueño georgiano
Georgian Dream
Грузинская мечта

Table of Contents

1. SOMNIUM

Every truly great adventure begins with a dream. When on a dark, sleepless night, trying to sleep, you are haunted by black thoughts of the frailty and despair of your life. The meaninglessness and emptiness of everything going on. Tiredness and irritation with everything around you. From people, dirty streets, aggression and anger, monstrous slavery and poverty, which soaked everything around you, reflected in the faces of people you are sick and tired of. To be more precise, it is not the people who are sickening, but what they have become. Stupefied by propaganda and eternal competition with each other. Stupidity and ignorance, aggression and malice, rudeness and permissiveness, lack of empathy and culture, total infantilization and degradation and grayness. You get very tired of it all. At some point it becomes simply unbearable to be in this country and in this place. And at that very moment there is a burning desire to leave it as soon as possible. It's like a needle piercing you with this feeling, taking over your thoughts and dreams, becoming an obsession and at the same time an obsession.

For, as the classic said: "For a real escape, you need to imagine and firmly know not where you are running to, but from whom and from where".

So I decided to go on a journey.

Thinking briefly, having mapped out the route, having a dream and a desperate desire to leave R, I decided to go to the fabulous and majestic Georgia.

Having sketched out a rough plan, prepared maps and routes, gathered the necessary things and said goodbye to my friends, I decided to set off.

My plan was to drive through the whole country, taking the most interesting and picturesque places along the way.

I was drawn to ancient castles and fortresses, majestic mountains and waterfalls, canyons and caves, seas and lakes, and everything I had once dreamed of visiting and seeing, enjoying the peace and quiet of unspoiled nature. But most importantly, on this journey, I wanted to feel the air of freedom again and breathe it fully, while being high up in the mountains. Because at that moment in time I was in a very stuffy place, where almost everything was saturated with violence and slavery, and I had to leave that place as soon as possible. Looking ahead, we will say that we managed to do it immediately after crossing the border, but we will have time to tell about it in detail and describe our feelings.

And I, not thinking long, started packing. I bought all the tickets, agreed with my colleagues about a long-term vacation, said goodbye to my friends and postponed all the business and projects until better times.

I decided to go through the city of Stavropol, which I really liked for its convenient location, clean streets, smiling people on the streets, warm and comfortable climate, beautiful views and a variety of destinations to which you could go through it. Plus flying to it was quite fast and inexpensive. In the end it all worked out that way, but not without excesses and complications, which I will have time to talk about in this essay.

Waking up early in the morning after a restless sleep, Ilya did not turn into a beetle, as in the well-known story. Although deep down I still dreamed about it, but this is another story, about which we will tell a little later.

So here it is. Waking up early in the morning, having collected the necessary things, I went to the airport. Having called a cab in advance, which arrived quickly and promptly enough. It was six in the morning and the city was just waking up. It was the perfect time to hit the road. A white company car pulled up, driven by a heavy driver, who sniffed and grunted nervously all the way, which was a little embarrassing, but after a while I got over it and didn't pay attention. While I was driving, I even had a wild thought in my head that it's people like that who have heart failure at the most crucial moment. From fatigue, excessive smoking and other reasons, which, in fact, did not matter much, because you have already imagined on the way, as he falls head on the steering wheel, and the car at full speed is carried to the pole, but it did not happen, although the anxiety increased with every kilometer of the way. It was all right. We arrived quickly enough. The airport was still relatively empty, and it was not difficult to check in for the flight, although boarding the plane was not without the excesses inherent in such flights. One of the passengers was not allowed to board the flight because of the size of his luggage and his laptop, which he was not allowed to take into the cabin. Because of this incident, of course, he made a big scandal and got into a fight with all the airport staff, even had to call the police, who calmed him down, which soon arrived, and I hope that he still flew away, because the reason was insignificant, and the cause was negligible.

The flight was smooth and quick enough, considering also that I took with me on the journey a fine book, consisting of two fine novels by the Marquis de Sade and Louis Breton, in which two immortal novels by the great creators of French diction. "Justine" and "Anti-Justine."

Reading on the airplane was very exciting and interesting. At some point I even had a thought in my head that I would read the book quickly enough, but this thought quickly disappeared, I looked at the passing clouds outside the window and in between we had already arrived in Stavropol.

2. STAVROPOL

As expected, the weather was beautiful. The sunshine and warm air reminded me of the ongoing summer, although in these parts it was not surprising.

The car to Batumi was not due until the evening, so I went for a walk in the city I had grown to love, enjoying the warm breeze and the unusually clean streets of this beautiful city. There were still plenty of places and sights I wanted to visit, so I went straight to them.

Not for nothing, after all, in the very center of the city there is a monument to the former mayor. It is true that under his careful leadership the city was recognized many times as the most comfortable and clean in Russia, which, of course, was reflected on the faces of local residents, who shone with smiles and serenity, even despite the fact that many were actively invited to the war, which continues for the second year for what reason and why. But let's not go into politics here, for there are enough people who will tell and write about it in detail without me.

Meanwhile, I will continue my narrative.

After walking around the city center, visiting all those places I wanted to visit, tasting local food, I came at the appointed hour to the bus stop, where, as I hoped, a bus should have been waiting for me. However, it was not as easy as I had hoped. It was nearing 7 p.m., and the bus should have been waiting for me. But, as often happens in my life, no one was waiting for me. Not thinking long, I called the driver, luckily his number was written on the ticket. The first time I dialed the number, the caller was unavailable. Notes of panic and despair passed in my soul, and I began to get nervous, but by a happy coincidence in five minutes I received a text message that the subscriber was back online. In my soul again appeared hope, I called again, and this time I was already answered.

Sergei answered, that was the driver's name, although nothing in his voice did not give away Sergei, rather, it was the voice of Ashot from the local market, selling watermelons, but, as I expected, he began to apologize to me, telling stories about how expensive the car was to him and how by an inexplicable coincidence of circumstances it suddenly refused to go. So he immediately offered me two options. Either his acquaintance would take me to Tbilisi, but already at ten at night, or he would take me for the same money, but tomorrow.

Not thinking long, I chose the second option, although it entailed money costs and unforeseen expenses, plus the thought that staying in Stavropol for one more day was not such a bad idea. The weather was fine, the nights were warm, and staying an extra day always promised new acquaintances and interesting stories. So I decided to stay in this clean and beautiful city for one more night, to leave the next day.

As subsequent events showed, this decision was quite reasonable and justified. All the more so because I quickly found a hostel nearby, and they just had a vacant place. As a rule, such forced stops are always fraught with interesting acquaintances, which later only proved to be true.

In the end, not far from the bus station, a room was found for me. In a beautiful and picturesque place, where a smiling and kind hostess was waiting for me, who not only showed me everything, but even provided me with a charger for my phone, because mine was no longer suitable for local sockets for some unknown reason, which did not cause any great inconvenience, although everything had to them. At the same time, the hostel had smiling and friendly guests. They not only engaged me in an interesting conversation, but also dispelled my anxieties, telling me over a mug of beer many interesting stories that happened to them during their frenetic travels in Turkey and near Asia, which they loved and revered.

Particularly zealous in his stories was a certain David, who, when asked what he was doing, always kept silent or simply said it was unimportant. At the same time, all his manners and phrases gave him away as a big boss of a tourist company, which he considered large enough to lead a serene life and build a string of his few subordinates.

Anyway, I figured him out quickly, though it wasn't the most difficult task. But all that was unimportant, much more interesting were his stories of amazing and desperate travels, which he told with enthusiasm, spitting saliva and pouring beer. By midnight we were joined by a lovely lady who had decided to get away from her tyrant parents and hide out in this place for a while. She also told us some fascinating stories from her childhood, which were one more horrific than the other.

In general, the evening flew by, and, decently intoxicated from drinking beer, we all went to bed, wishing each other good night.

I should say at once that nights in such places, especially when subconsciously still a little nervous about unfinished business, are not easy for me. I often can't sleep all night or fall asleep only in the morning, only to wake up soon after. At the same time I often have very vivid but short dreams in which I see myself either in the past or in the distant future, which sooner or later catches up with me. Often these are peculiar omens born from the dark depths of the subconscious, which reflect all my fears and experiences, drawing me into their surreal worlds, often with a very violent and unexpected ending, which like a flash flash flash through my memory, leaving deep wounds on my heart and in the depths of my soul. Although I do not think that everything will be exactly like that and as tragic, but often they do come true, which leaves wounds on my heart that bleed from time to time. That restless night I dreamt of fear and despair, represented in the form of energy beings and fairy tale manifestations that I had never seen before, which struck me with their realism and spongy structure, taking on unimaginable forms. The dream was short, though very vivid, and I awoke quite early. And as soon as I woke up, I immediately wanted to leave the place as soon as possible without leaving any trace of my being there.

So eventually I did.

Having had a good breakfast, I went in search of unexplored places that I had not yet seen. And I still found them, loving this glorious city of Stavropol even more, which revived in my soul faith in people, nothing less. It was still necessary to try to do this, because everyone knows me as a desperate and strict critic of our tragic reality, and I dare say that it is quite justified, because I have been many places and seen a lot of things both in Russia and abroad. But, having come to this city, I again believed in people, in their sincerity and beauty, in the boldness of smiles and display of sincere emotions without a share of falsity and pretentiousness, which is typical of people from big cities in this country.

In general, I walked until the evening, not thinking about time and inconvenience, which in any case seemed to be part of a great adventure.

I didn't even notice when the clock struck six o'clock in the evening and the long-awaited minibus was waiting for me, which would finally take me to Georgia.

3. ROAD

This time he did pull up. A white Mercedes, comfortable enough to accommodate six people. What really surprised me was not the car itself, because I had traveled in such cars before, but its driver Sergey, who turned out to be a very charismatic and interesting person. And I think that it is definitely worth saying a few words about him, for he definitely deserves attention. He was stocky, strong build, black-haired, and masculine in appearance, he had a great sense of humor, but, like all his colleagues in the role, a sense of musical taste, he was not distinguished. All the way he played Georgian and Russian popular songs, but very rarely, but still there were interesting compositions, which even surprised me. He was short and looked more like a dwarf from a David Lynch movie, except that he was not wearing a red jacket, instead he wore a black leather jacket, which only emphasized his charisma and gave him confidence.

He told me right away that first of all, he was filling in for the driver who was originally supposed to take us. Secondly, he would take us only to Tbilisi, after which we would be taken to Batumi by his friends, for whom we would wait no more than ten minutes. Thirdly, on the way we had to pick up an Armenian who was going to Azerbaijan, and an Azerbaijani who was going to Armenia, which seemed strange to me, and three other girls from different cities, and one of them would be pregnant, so he would put her in the front seat next to him.

In general, I immediately realized that the trip is expected to be difficult, which was later confirmed, but we will have time to talk about it here.

Anyway, we drove off. Sergey pressed the gas pedal and started driving, and at once quite fast and confidently. I immediately realized that he knows the route well and drives people along it quite regularly, and if some time ago I had some excitement, it soon disappeared.

Not an hour into the trip, we stopped to pick up the first passengers I mentioned earlier. They were: a bald and stocky Armenian of about fifty years old and an Azerbaijani similar to him. I even thought for a moment that they were brothers, because they looked so much alike. But later I discarded this thought. Still, judging by their communication, I assumed that they were at least good friends.

An hour or three later we reached the first stop, which was Mineralnye Vody, and it was in this town that we were to pick up the first passenger.

She was a middle-aged girl, of athletic build, with a distinct Belarusian accent, a little rude in appearance, but at the same time quite friendly and sociable, which all together gave her away as an avid traveler. Later it was confirmed in the conversations we had during the whole trip. As it turned out, she was traveling to Tbilisi.

After getting into the car in the back seat next to me, we immediately began a relaxed conversation. As it is customary for all desperate travelers, sharing plans, stories, directions and routes.

Time flies by in such moments, especially when you have something to say and tell, and we had enough stories that were more interesting than each other. Soon we arrived in Pyatigorsk, where the next travel companion was waiting for us. Her name was Svetlana, and she too, like me, was going to Batumi. Later we will have a separate adventure with her, which I will have time to tell you about.

Svetlana, by the way, was no less sociable girl, so there were more stories in the back seat, but at the same time there were more anxieties and worries, which are typical for such trips. After about an hour we stopped again to pick up the last passenger, who quickly enough settled into the seat next to the driver and took the last available seat.

The car was fully packed and we were off, and quite quickly and confidently at that. This time we could not read on the way, because it got dark very quickly, and conversations on the way were quite active, so we did not get bored. At the same time it was impossible to sleep too, because bumps and bumps on the road constantly woke me up, not letting me sleep. And the way was long and tiring enough, especially for the girls, who were obviously not used to such trips, so they periodically complained and worried about everything in the world. But not me. For me, such trips are always exciting and interesting, just like the views from the window and the feeling of the journey that just takes your breath away. I had traveled by bus and car many times before, so this trip was quite familiar to me, especially in such a company and with such interesting fellow travelers. Five hours later we were already at the border, which, by the way, we passed quickly enough. Everyone's documents were in order, and the border guards did not ask any unnecessary questions. There were not so many cars traveling that night as usual, so in half an hour we were in Georgia. And here the most interesting thing started. Incredible joy and enthusiasm flared up in my soul. The feeling of freedom and mountain air inspired me so much that I didn't want to sleep. Although it was already dark night, and almost nothing was visible, but thanks to the illumination some parts of the mountains looked just amazing. Serpentines, mountain roads, passing trucks - all together tsave a huge dose of adrenaline and caused genuine interest. Meanwhile, it was already three o'clock in the morning, and I began to notice how all the passengers began to fall into sleep. All except me, the driver and the girl sitting next to him, who had already managed to talk to the driver during the journey, and they had become so close that he let her not only play her favorite songs, but also hold the steering wheel when he needed to be distracted by an urgent call. Which was a little dangerous, though it was obvious from her confident movements that it wasn't the first time she'd done it. After a while, when the first snoring was heard in the cabin, I began to notice how the driver's conversations with the girl sitting next to him became quite indecent. He allowed her both dirty jokes and obscene compliments, which was a bit unusual, because I had never met such impudence before. It came to the point that at some point we stopped at a hotel where we could spend the night and rent a room, which was not convenient and did not fit into the itinerary. However, when I heard our driver's frank and impudent suggestion to the girl sitting next to him to get out quickly, have sex in the hotel and come back, at that moment I immediately understood everything. He was already so excited and heated that he was ready to rape her, even in the bushes, even in the hotel, especially since he was sure that everyone was already asleep and would not notice anything. But a ringing and whip slap cooled him down quickly, waking up all the passengers. After that, our driver had no choice but to continue the journey and drown out all the lustful and lecherous thoughts. I, as always, could not fall asleep and watched the scene, which amused and surprised me at the same time.

I had never seen anything like it before, but I had never even considered that it could happen. This scene was more like an episode of a movie or series that is on TV every day. And we continued on our way. Sergey was clearly taken aback by such an unexpected refusal, so he pressed the gas pedal even harder and drove even faster, which was not quite justified, given the winding and dangerous parts of the road. It was noticeable that such a refusal clearly annoyed him, and even for a moment it seemed that he had nothing to lose, but responsibility and professionalism prevailed over him, and after a while he calmed down. Eventually our trip continued, and after a couple hours it became much brighter. All of us watched a beautiful dawn, which in the mountains acquires a special, incomparable charm, inflaming the soul with joy and barely noticeable anxiety about the upcoming impressions.

4. TBILISI - ADVENTURES ON THE WAY TO BATUMI

At six o'clock in the morning we were already in Tbilisi. Everyone was exhausted and tired, that's why the dialogs were quite sluggish and sleepy, which did not embarrass me at all, because I had been preparing myself for this for a long time. Even more, I prepared myself for this all summer, desperately looking for companions and companions, but never found anyone, which at first caused sadness and sadness, but when I arrived in Georgia, I realized that it is much better, and companions will always find me. After all, there were plenty of such lonely travelers at all times, and impressions and amazing stories in the country I love will appear by themselves, because people in Georgia are very hospitable and friendly, which is so rare to find in modern Russia, and that is why I ran away from everyone far away. I felt at home the very first moment I was here. And this incomparable feeling of love and kindness, hospitality and support, and it doesn't matter where you come from, the main thing is to remain a human being in any, even the most difficult and dangerous situation. You would know how much I miss this in Russia, although people close and familiar to me understand it very well, and it is often the topic of many of our conversations with friends or people I know.

As it turned out, we arrived much earlier than planned. The first passengers were about to get off, and I felt an elusive sadness in my soul, because we had already become friends and had communicated very warmly all the way, but we had to say goodbye. But it was just a thought. I hugged everyone who was leaving, only Svetlana was left, who, like me, was going to Batumi.

We arrived early, so while we were waiting for the bus, we even had time to sleep a little. To tell you the truth, I even had a dream. In my dream I dreamed as if I was in paradise, among paradise bushes and marvelous landscapes, where a melody so beautiful and pleasant to my ear was playing that I still consider it the most important and interesting dream of my whole life. There was a very sweet and pleasant ambient sound in the garden of Eden. Lyre sounds overlaid with airy and light electronics. I couldn't believe my ears. It was truly heavenly music, which I had never heard in my life until now, although all many people know me as a collector of the most bizarre and strange sounds, which I have been searching all my life, looking for all the strangest and most amazing things, discovering new worlds and horizons in sound.

In general, the dream was simply magical, and I will remember it many times in the future, sharing impressions and new discoveries with both friends and people I know.

And at this late hour, finishing the last glass of divine Pirosmani, I remember this dream, which evoked so many emotions and wonderful memories in me.

I was awakened by a light pat on my shoulder. Our bus to Batumi had pulled up, and we had to get on our way. I quickly ran to the currency exchanger to exchange some rubles for local lari, although the rate was not favorable at all, but, as it turned out later, it was the right decision, which will help me later, but I will have time to tell you about it here.

So, we moved, said goodbye to everyone who was going to other regions, and set off on the route from Tbilisi to Batumi. We had to drive for six hours, but I did not care about the time, because I was already tired, and I had only one thought - to get there as soon as possible.

There was a minibus full of people, but what kind of people they were, I had yet to find out. Here I will tell only about those with whom I managed to communicate and get acquainted.

So, besides Svetlana, there were two Georgian girlfriends of eighteen years old, cheerful and carefree, which immediately caught my eye. One of them could easily fall in love with me, but I understood perfectly well that fate would separate us, although a little later I managed to communicate with her a little. There was also a group of sportsmen friends, a Georgian guy whose name was Rizo, by the way, we immediately found a common language with him. There were also a few women who got off on the way, and a second driver who smoked cigarettes right in the cabin, one after another during the whole trip. The journey was not a long one, but incredibly fascinating, which I will have time to tell you more about. All the way I could not sleep a wink, for the views outside the window exceeded all my expectations. Majestic mountains, thick fog on many peaks, waterfalls, canyons, castles and fortresses high in the mountains, picturesque villages on the slopes and countless tunnels that penetrated the mountains through and through. Tunnels that were built in huge numbers along the way. I can only imagine how easy and comfortable it will be to travel through the most seemingly inaccessible mountain sections, which previously could only be reached on foot or on horseback, but technology is advancing, and the road through the mountains, once seemingly impossible, is becoming incredibly exciting and interesting. We were approaching the fifth hour of the journey. At the same time we stopped many times in very beautiful places, which was already invigorating and joyful at the same time. At that moment the first drops of rain started to drip on the glass. It would seem that there was nothing unusual about it, but later I realized that not everything was so simple. As the ride was about to end and the rain was getting heavier, I noticed that the driver had turned off the route. Everyone suddenly got out and started talking loudly about something in Georgian. Svetlana and I were a little confused, but later, when we got out, we were told that all the roads on the way to Batumi were flooded, there was a strong storm, and we would not be able to go any further. I looked at the map, we were in a place called Lanchkhuti, at the railroad station. The nearest train to Batumi would pass by only at seven in the evening, and it was about one o'clock in the afternoon.

The station we were forced to stop at was a rather pathetic sight. There were dilapidated Soviet-built walls and dogs everywhere, of which there are quite a few in Georgia. They are always hungry, but they are friendly and do not bother tourists. They live so well here that they either sleep in the shade or lie on their backs, paws up, with a blissful smile on their faces. There were plenty of them in this place, too. There were still some sweet waffles in my backpack, and I shared them with them, to the dogs' delight, even though I was already very hungry. That's why they followed me around in packs. One dog even got up on his hind legs and jumped around me, trying to beg for another waffle, so I gave him the last one as a reward for his tricks.

The only other person besides us at this station was an elderly female cashier who was very nice to us, spoke good Russian and answered all our questions. So we settled down on a bench nearby and started waiting for the train. And at that moment it turned out that many of the people who were traveling with us spoke excellent Russian. Thanks to this I got to know everyone better, especially Rizo, about whom I have already written here and who turned out to be a great guy. As he told me, he was taught Russian by his father, who had once served in the Russian armed forces. He had instilled in him a love of Russian language and literature, thanks to which he told us some interesting stories. In general, we were not bored, and after a while the rain began to subside, and with it came some good news. In half an hour a train was going to pass by, which was going to Ureki, and from there it was quite easy to get to Batumi. So we took the news with considerable enthusiasm, especially Svetlana, who was the most tired of all. Besides, she called her friend who kindly agreed to pick us up from Ureki by car and take us to Batumi, which was not too far away. He was also not against taking Rizo with us for company. He was going to Kabuleti, which was on the way. Meanwhile, the train was on its way, we promptly bought tickets and went to the platform. While we were walking, the train was already approaching. We took our comfortable seats and drove off, happy with the fact that we were so fortunate. We reached Ureki quite quickly. A car was waiting for us there, and having promptly moved to the back seat, we drove to Batumi. Behind the window we could see incredibly beautiful mountains and waterfalls. Passing by Mtirala reserve, which was located on the mountain of the same name, I was amazed by its variety of vegetation and "cap" of fog, which looked very picturesque. It is not for nothing that locals call this mountain "weeping", as it is foggy here almost all year round. All this caused incomparable emotions and feelings of happiness and joy. Soon we were already in Batumi. On the way we said goodbye to Rizo, who went to Kabuleti. After exchanging phone numbers with everyone, saying goodbye warmly and wishing good luck, I went to look for my hotel.

5. BATUMI - FORTRESS OF GONIO

On the way, I immediately felt and sensed the local atmosphere. The streets were as crowded as always, because Batumi has long been famous as a city of real travelers, with people from all over the world. There was a sense of freedom so strong in the air that I immediately felt at home. The views of the sea and the city were fantastic. Modern architecture here was juxtaposed with majestic monuments of both early and late medieval times. I was especially impressed by the Gonio Fortress, which was not far from the city. Passing by, I decided to visit it.

Erected by the ancient Romans, more than two thousand years ago, it fully symbolized the greatness and power of the ancient Roman Empire and at the same time the genius of Roman engineers, thanks to which its walls are perfectly preserved. On its territory are still excavated, which have revealed to the world many secrets and unique treasures, which are all collected in the local museum. Its walls are beautifully preserved. Carefully built of black volcanic stone, they were strong enough to repel enemy attacks for hundreds of years. While I was exploring it, I joined a Russian tour group who were exploring the local sights as I was. From their guide I learned that the first mention of this fortress belonged to Pliny the Younger at the beginning of the first century AD. In the second century there was already a well-fortified Roman city on this place, and the fortress was a kind of military base, and it was here that the eastern border of the Roman Empire passed, which made it an important strategic point. The fortress helped to protect the entrances to the gorge of the Chorokhi and Acharistskali rivers and performed an important defensive function. From 1547 to 1878 the fortress belonged to the Ottoman Empire, and after the peace in the Russo-Turkish war it became part of the Russian Empire.

The full name of the fortress is Gonio-Apsaros, and there is a legend that this prefix through a dash is related to the ancient Greek myth of the Argonauts. Allegedly, it was here that the son of the Colchian king Apsyrtes, who was killed by Jason, was buried.

Walking around the territory of the fortress, I noticed an interesting grave, and as the tourists from the group told me later, its secret is that, according to legend, Matvei - one of the 12 apostles of Jesus Christ - is buried there. There is a hypothesis that after the death of his teacher he came here to preach. But it is not possible to be 100%

sure of this, as the Georgian government has banned any excavations near the tomb. But the legend is interesting in any case.

I was also interested in the preserved remains of the sewage system of those times and the pipeline, which was used to supply hot water for important gentlemen, preheated over fire in large vats.

After wandering around for a few more hours, I went in search of my hotel. It was located in the very center of the city, near Europe Square, within walking distance of the sea and all the sights. I quickly threw off my things, had a snack and went for a walk along the beautiful promenade, which at night amazed by the brightness of colors and the abundance of tourists from all over the world.

I came to the hotel at midnight. Tired, but very satisfied, I quickly fell asleep, immediately falling into a deep sleep.

That was how my first day went, and my adventure was just beginning.

The next day I had planned a trip to Zugdidi, but the changeable weather made a change. From the very morning it rained heavily, which according to the forecast was supposed to end only by the evening. After walking around for a while and getting soaked to the skin, I decided to postpone the trip to the next day. After spending half a day at the hotel reading "Antigustine" and chatting with the hotel guests, I didn't get out for a walk until the evening, going to a part of the city I hadn't had a chance to visit yet. I ended up having a great time enjoying the architectural masterpieces and beautiful views that awaited me at every turn.

Already closer to the night I called my friends whom I had not seen for a long time. It was very pleasant for me to meet them in Batumi. We had dinner and spent a wonderful evening for warm conversations and walks, and at night we even managed to visit a music festival, which pleased me very much with interesting music and good atmosphere. Even the dogs were dancing that night, which proved once again that I was in the right place at the right time. I arrived at the hotel quite late, which, however, did not prevent me from planning the next day and getting a good night's sleep, because I had big plans.

6. ZUGDIDI - DADIANI PALACE

The next day I set off to Zugdidi from the very morning. The bus station was half an hour's walk from my hotel, and as I approached it I met Gennady, who was an experienced driver and regularly took people along this route. He left me his phone number in case I got lost somewhere and asked me to call him in case I got lost so he could take me back. It was not a long drive, about three hours, passing such towns as Kobuleti, Poti, Ureki, which were very beautiful in their own way, so the trip flew by unnoticed.

When I arrived in Zugdidi, I immediately went to the Dadiani Palace, which I had wanted to visit for a long time. Made in medieval style, it was very beautiful and well preserved. It was the ancient residence of the Mingrelian rulers, who had always taken good care of it. Built of good stone, which allowed it to be well preserved until today.

Its history began in 1837, when by the command of Prince David Dadiani temporary palaces were erected in Zugdidi, which later turned into modern residences. In the 60s of the XIX century they were replaced by the two-storeyed Royal Palace, and in the 1880s next to it appeared the presentable palace of Niko Dadiani, built by Russian architect Leonid Vasiliev. It is also distinguished by its spectacular classical architecture, which surprisingly combines imperial and national motifs of Georgian architecture. Arched windows, arched openings, original turrets on the roof, stucco reliefs on the walls - all this, in my opinion, allows to call the palace one of the most beautiful buildings in Georgia. The interiors of the buildings looked no less gorgeous, especially the outer gallery, the wooden ceilings of which look like true works of man-made art. Their figurative curls and ornaments look harmoniously against the background of simple, rough columns and are well combined with carved doors, metal candlesticks, furniture sets made by masters of the French school of the XIX century.

I also decided to take a look at its decoration. Once inside, I was simply amazed by the abundance of finds and unique things. As the local guide told me, during the construction of the complex, unique numismatic materials from the ancient city of Archaeopolis (nowadays Nokalakevi) were accidentally discovered on its territory. The findings served as a reason for the creation of its own museum, which was opened in the Royal Palace by the efforts of Prince David Dadiani. The museum fund includes more than 44 thousand exhibits dating from the I century BC to the XIX century of the modern era. In addition

to those ancient finds, countless other valuable objects and artifacts are presented within its walls. First of all, these are archaeological exhibits of the ancient Greek and Georgian period, Christian sacred relics, including the Holy Robe of the Mother of God, samples of European applied art, relics of the princes of Samegrelo and royal families of France, Russia, Spain, manuscripts of the XV-XIX centuries, Napoleon's and Dadiani's libraries, European and Asian weapons, a collection of paintings by Russian Peredvizhniki, French painters-batalists and English marine artists, a collection of photographs, crystal, porcelain and faience dishes. But the most important treasure of the museum is the posthumous mask of Napoleon, made of bronze after the death of the great emperor. As the same guide told me, three such masks were made - one of them is in a private collection, the second one is kept in the church of Misericordia on the island of Elba, and the third one was given to Georgia by the descendants of Murat, who owned the Dadiani Palace for some time. Leaving the palace, it was difficult for me to ignore the brilliant Botanical Garden, spread around the palace on an area of 26.4 hectares. This paradise, created in the middle of the XIX century, owes its appearance to Ekaterina Chavchavadze-Dadiani (David's wife), who sent experienced gardeners from Europe to create the park area. The princess was enthusiastic about her work and in a short time filled the garden with many exotic plants. Today it counts more than 80 species of flora, brought to the territory of Georgia from the countries of South-East Asia, India, Japan, the Mediterranean and America. I was especially struck by its layout, in which the hand of a real genius of landscape design of a bygone era was noticeable. Having had a little rest and a good look around, I set out for the city. Walking through its streets, I suddenly noticed familiar faces. It was an Armenian and an Azerbaijani, with whom I was traveling from Stavropol. By the will of fate they were passing through Zugdidi. We immediately recognized each other and got to talking. I was very surprised to meet them here.

While we were chatting, they told me an interesting story about the palace, the garden and the nearby mountain streams, to which they regularly went to relax and improve their health. They were very close to the city, and passing through it, as the legend goes, one could come out young and beautiful. I appreciated their sense of humor, but I didn't check it, I didn't have time for it, but I liked the story very much. Soon I said goodbye to them. Wishing them a wonderful experience, I went on my way. After walking for a couple more hours, I suddenly remembered that my friends invited me to a concert, which was to be in Batumi in the evening, so I quickly went to the bus station. I even got a little lost on the way, which, however, did not upset me much, because in the distance I could see a very picturesque landscape, which was pleasant to admire. So I found the right road and came to the appointed hour, where Gennady was already waiting for me and other passengers. After a while we already drove back to Batumi on the same road.

7. BATUMI - FURTHER ADVENTURES

Having arrived quickly enough, I immediately went to the address given to me by my friends for the supposed concert. At least, I thought it was supposed to be a concert, but it turned out to be not quite so. Suffice it to say that the place where it was held was unusual and highly underground. The club was called "Giggles", and its outlines were painfully familiar. There are still quite a few such clubs in St. Petersburg, especially in the center, so it felt as if I had traveled back in time and space. But all this was fleeting, for the events overwhelmed me upon arrival. The audience was mostly Russian-speaking. For the most part they were either fugitive artists and musicians, or casual travelers, or ordinary tourists who came to pass the evening.

Once there, I was immediately drawn to a lecture on the partisan movement during World War II. Which was fascinating and interesting in its own way. Of course, I did not learn anything new in it, because I had been interested in this subject before. I often enough resorted to it during my intellectual searches and research. The most interesting was still ahead of me.

After the end of the lecture I went out into the courtyard, where I met a very motley crowd. Especially there were a lot of travelers, who, just like me, were traveling in Georgia. Against this background we all got to know each other and chatted for about half an hour on various topics. The evening was warm, so I enjoyed every minute of it.

For a while I even forgot where I was and it felt like I was back in good old Peter. There are more than enough such places and companies there, and such events take place quite often. But let's not stray far from the topic.

After the lecture there was an interesting conversation between modern partisans and those people who sympathized with them,

shared stories from their lives and collected donations for Ukrainian refugees who were forced to flee from the war going on in their country.

The time was already approaching midnight. Everyone was waiting for the concert. There was a band called "Magic Single Cell Music" that I was already quite familiar with, having been to their concerts many times. The fact that they were performing in Batumi that day surprised me very much. Looking ahead, I can safely say that the concert was a success. It was real and the best version of kraut-rock at its best. Nowadays you could rarely meet such kind of rock, especially in Georgia.

So I was incredibly glad to be in this place at this hour. I enjoyed the music very much, and a couple hours of the concert flew by unnoticed. The day was coming to an end, and I went to bed, for my adventure was just beginning, and I had a long way to go.

It is also worth mentioning that while talking to my friends, I unwittingly, or maybe even quite deliberately, shared my plans for my adventures in the coming days. I was planning to visit many more cities, and the road ahead was not easy. All my friends were very supportive and encouraged me in every possible way, giving me a handful of magic capsules to support me and give me the necessary strength for my adventure. The capsules contained concentrated and powdered red fly agaric, collected in the distant Siberian forests. As I understood it, it had recently become particularly popular in the creative community, and was used by many for work and a little for pleasure.

By taking a capsule before a responsible work or event, concentration improves and strength stays, which sets you up well for the desired result. Nature itself gives us strength, and who are we not to use its gifts? And, as it turned out later, the capsules helped me a lot, preventing me from getting very tired on the road, while maintaining full concentration and attention.

As I wrote earlier, my hotel, where I stayed, was very close to the sea, which gave it an advantage over all the others. But to find it, I had to go through a narrow street and turn into a courtyard. I didn't always get there the first time, so sometimes I had to wander around and waste time looking for it. That night I didn't find her right away, which didn't stop me from getting a good night's sleep.

I woke up early enough by local standards, at seven o'clock in the morning, when the city was just waking up, and the local fruit sellers were just starting to arrange ripe fruits on the counter. The road led me to the ancient city of Akhaltsikhe.

8. AKHALTSIKHE

This city was located in the very south of Georgia. Located on the Potskhovi River, which in turn was the left tributary of the Kura River, Akhaltsikhe was once the center of culture and arts, politics and economy of the Meskhetian region. Also, long ago, the city was the seat of the Jakeli family, who for five hundred years were the most powerful political force in South Georgia.

Frankly speaking, I didn't know much about Akhaltsikhe, so while riding in the bus, I diligently filled up my knowledge about this ancient place, which fascinated me for the next six hours.

What attracted me to this place, first of all, was Akhaltsikhe fortress, which has always been a world historical landmark, an ancient monument of both Georgian and Ottoman empires. Since the 12th century, these two great kingdoms had been at war with each other and there was a fierce struggle on this territory all the time. It needed very powerful, strong defenses and strong walls to withstand the onslaught of the enemy, so I was not at all surprised when I saw it all with my own eyes. Touching and staying in such ancient historical places always gave me strength and impressions. Looking ahead, I will say that everything was more than justified, and I had a wonderful time there.

I arrived in the afternoon, when the sun was shining brightly and the air had already warmed up enough to make my forehead evaporate. Along the way, I passed dozens of tunnels that cut through the mountains, shortening the distance between towns and cities. As we drove along, I couldn't take my eyes off the beautiful and majestic mountain peaks, waterfalls and mountain rivers. I was simply amazed by their power and beauty. The whole road was one continuous adventure, that's why I always say that traveling by car is a great pleasure, and I never understood people who fear or dread it.

The day, as I wrote above, was simply beautiful and the sun was shining blindingly bright. When I arrived in Akhaltsikhe I immediately decided to walk around the city, for it was beautiful and amazing in its own way. In the very center of the city, on the square, there was a huge monument to Queen Tamara, which looked very impressive and stunned me with its size. I immediately thought how lucky the people were to be ruled by such a majestic and wise woman. Although she ruled many centuries ago, but the time of her rule is still considered a golden age in the history of the Georgian kingdom. And the monument itself was in good condition, which only convinced me in the thought, along with other facts that in this small town lives a lot of decent and kind people. This fact, later confirmed, during my short stay, I walked around the city for a few hours and, a little later, went to look for my new home.

I will say at once that it was in a marvelous, very convenient and picturesque place. The majestic fortress was very close by. I was received and welcomed very cordially. The hostess was a very nice and friendly woman, who spoke excellent Russian and at first sight disposed to kindness and comfort. At the same time, she was an excellent cook and made me a very hearty and tasty lunch. After a little rest, I went to Akhaltsikhe fortress. A little bit of history, really, about it is worth telling. The original name of the fortress in the 9th century was Lomsia, which translates from Georgian as lion, at the end of the twelfth century Lomsia acquired a new name Akhaltsikhe, which literally translates as "New Fortress". One of the modern names "Rabat" is of Jewish/Arabic origin and means any fortified place. Usually, this was the name of the commercial quarter of the fortress, previously the Rabat area was inhabited mainly by Jewish merchants and artisans, but the name gradually stuck to the fortress itself, strictly formally Rabat is considered to be the part of Akhaltsikhe, which is located on the height of the fortress.

Approaching it, I immediately felt the magnitude and power of this ancient place, especially since it was recently reconstructed and restored, being in very good condition. The size and thickness of the walls, the gates and watchtowers, everything was a real delight.

In the very center of the fortress was the castle of Jakeli, which stood on a small hill. There was also a Christian temple next to it. Besides, on the territory of the fortress there was a court, an arsenal, a mint, a bathhouse, a mosque in the style of the Byzantine Orthodox Church, in which, as they say, once upon a time there was one of the richest libraries of the Muslim East. There was also a tunnel leading to the Potskhovi River, which, however, was temporarily closed. However, there were quite a lot of tourists on this day, especially from China and the Czech Republic, which only brightened up the day and diluted the atmosphere.

Walking through the garden inside the fortress, past the amphitheater, examining the mosque, I never ceased to marvel at the history and antiquity of this beautiful monument to bygone eras, majestic nations and fierce battles that have not stopped in these places at all times. Nowadays, it has turned into a historical monument and one of the main attractions of both Georgia and the whole region, which only adorns this quiet and small town.

Having explored everything well and in detail, I headed for the exit, walking one last time along the walls of the fortress and enjoying the marvelous view that opens up from its high walls. On the way, I already met the first reflections of the sunset, which, with its delicate peach hues saturated my eyes and left in my soul very warm and colorful memories.

Having bought on the way a bottle of good wine from the local wineries, I decided to celebrate this beautiful and intense day and to start making the first notes for this manuscript, which I still continued, trying to note in detail all the events and emotions that visited me.

When I began my work on the text, I immediately noted how easy and inspired I felt to write in this wonderful place. When strong red wine gives contrasts, and the mountain air saturates your blood with oxygen, and all the darkness and horror are left far behind. When no one distracts you with their petty problems, when no one knocks on the door, when the phone doesn't ring, when you don't have to rush to work, when you don't have to watch the weather outside the window, when you don't have to call anyone, when you don't have to meet your friends, when you don't have to cook, when you don't have to go shopping, when you don't have to stand in lines, when you don't have to get wet in the rain, when you don't have to read bad news and there are no other news, when you don't have to react to countless events, when you don't have to hurry, when you don't have to run, when you don't have to go to someone, when you don't have to explain something to someone, when you don't have to draw anything, when you don't have to listen to anyone, when you don't have to scold anyone, when you don't have to be angry with anyone, when you don't have to complain to anyone, when you don't have to hit anyone, when you don't have to instruct anyone, when you don't have to tell anyone anything, when you don't have to ask for anything, when you don't have to humiliate anyone, when you don't have to buy anything, when you don't have to go to bed, when you don't have to buy anything, when you don't have to watch for discounts, when you don't have to watch for reactions, when you don't have to take pictures, when you don't have to wonder once again at the stupidity of people, when you don't have to compete with anyone, when you don't have to curse anyone, when you don't have to analyze, when you don't have to divide into parts, when you don't have to answer letters, when you don't have to sell anything, when you don't have to negotiate, when you don't have to go to court, to when you don't have to count minutes, when you don't have to water flowers, when you don't have to play the flute, when you don't have to take medicine, when you don't have to choose shoes, when you don't have to be afraid of water, when you don't have to take antidepressants, when you don't have to go to a psychologist, when you don't have to give interviews, when you don't have to answer questions, when you don't have to act in a movie, when you don't have to play tennis, when you don't have to choose songs for a radio show, when you don't have to dig through your notes, when you don't have to walk in the woods, when you don't have to pick mushrooms, when you don't have to go to Omsk, when you don't have to remember former friends and girlfriends, when you don't have to argue about the nature of color, when you don't have to berate yourself for having done something wrong in the past, when you don't have to do the dishes, when you don't have to wash dirty clothes, when you don't have to give flowers, when you don't have to sell vases, when you don't have to get fire, when you don't have to wait for help, when you don't have to worry about whether or not that your bookshelf is about to collapse under the weight of Montaigne and Rousseau, when you don't have to discuss the latest pranks of the old ghoul, when you don't have to discuss the latest conspiracy theories, when you don't have to argue with your neighbor about whether it's Botox or banquet or whether they forgot to defrost it, when you don't have to entertain the neighbor's cat, when you don't have to argue with your neighbors, when you don't have to pay your bills, when you don't have to complain about the fact when it gets dark very quickly, when you don't have to be upset that Annushka has already spilled oil, when you don't have to roast nuts, when you don't have to count the money in your pocket, when you don't have to hurry to English class, when you don't have to envy those who are lucky, when you don't have to win, when you don't have to lose, when you don't have to lie down, when you don't have to stand, when you don't have to talk, when you can just write for your own pleasure, when your soul just wants to fly. And it was at that moment that I realized that the eternal questions I had been asking myself all my life had not become smarter. That's why they're eternal. Maybe that's the point. Not to think where the way out is, but to realize that life is a crossroads where you are standing right now, then the labyrinth of meanings will disappear, because it exists only in our minds, and in reality, there is only a simple choice of where to go.

After a while, I began to notice that the bottle of wine was running out, and at that moment I heard someone calling me. I went out to look and saw the owner of the house and the hostess and her son calling me to join them for dinner. I did not disregard their hospitality and joined them, and I did not regret it at all. The food was very tasty, the fruit was ripe and sweet, and the local chacha was incredibly strong. The conversation was flowing, the table was bursting with delicious food, and surprisingly, I immediately found a common language with everyone. After all, intelligent and enlightened people always find something to talk about, and in this house others did not dwell, which pleased me very much. All present were interested in politics, art, music and movies. I, in turn, shared stories from the places I had visited, and in return I was told local legends and customs. Time flew by very quickly, and we parted almost in the morning, which did not prevent me from sleeping soundly and blissfully, having gained strength for the next adventure, which I was to have the next day, and the impressions awaited me no less amazing.

Having had a good breakfast in the morning, I bade farewell to all the inhabitants of this beautiful house, and set off for Borjomi.

9. BORJOMI

We didn't drive very long. It was only about three hours. I had stopped noticing such distances because of the beauty of the views and scenery outside the window, especially since I was absorbed in reading on the road, which accelerated the time even faster, and very soon we arrived at the local bus station. As soon as I got off the bus, I immediately felt the local air, which my friends and acquaintances had told me about before. It was very fresh, with light notes of sulfur and minerals, which in these parts were found not only in water, but also in some products. The view that presented itself to my eyes was very beautiful and peculiar. The majestic mountains that went beyond the horizon, the fog enveloping their tops, the mountain river that penetrated the city through, extensive vegetation and suspension bridges, which I had not seen so often before, but Borjomi was famous for them, thus attracting many tourists from all over the world. Not far from the bus station I immediately noticed a huge and very skillfully made monument to the great Russian composer Pyotr Ilyich Tchaikovsky. The monument was unusual in its own way and differed from many other monuments erected in his honor, seen by me in different parts of Russia. Here he was not sitting on a chair or bench, conducting an invisible orchestra, but stood leaning on a cane, and as if in a hurry, making a characteristic gesture with his right hand, as if the composer was warning someone against a rash and foolish act.

In general, I liked it immediately, especially since behind it there was a music school, from the windows of which the most beautiful music was always coming, which so pleasantly caressed my ears and encouraged me to new discoveries. In front of the monument there was also a small fountain, a public garden, and the place itself was very cozy and musical. Separately it is also worth mentioning a small plaque that was fixed on the wall of the music school. The text on it was written in Georgian and Russian, thanks to which I managed to read it. It was Tchaikovsky's famous phrase about Borjomi, which said: "One of the most beautiful places I have ever seen". I confess that this phrase was often in my head while I was a guest here, and I wanted to say it myself more than once and more than twice. After drinking water from the drinking fountain, which, by the way, were everywhere here, I went in search of my new home. Although it was very close by, it was not so easy to find. There were no signs, so I had to ask the locals, who kindly showed me the way and guided me to the right place. The hostess met me very cordially. She was a middle-aged Georgian woman whose name was Vaniko. She immediately showed me my room, kitchen and bathroom. Everything was neat and minimalistic. The house also had a spiral staircase that led to a terrace from which the panorama of this cozy and beautiful city was clearly visible. After throwing off my backpack and taking a shower, I set out to look for local attractions.

In the morning the locals had told me that there was a fortress in the suburbs, somewhere near the town, on a high mountain, which I was anxious to find. As I walked past the private houses and picked plums, which grew in abundance and fell on my head, I kept looking up at the mountain tops in the hope of finding it. It was not so easy, but the kind locals once again helped me and showed me the way. There was a narrow staircase leading to the fortress, which was located between the houses and went uphill. As I climbed higher and higher, I could already see the ruins of walls and towers. Soon I saw a sign with a detailed description of the fortress. It was "Gogia Fortress" or

Gogiastsikhe. By the way, it has been preserved rather poorly. Only the wall and one of the towers remained, but the view of the city and nearby settlements was fantastic. The city was like in the palm of your hand, you could see everything in the smallest detail. It had been built for this purpose a long time ago. The date of construction varies between the tenth and fourteenth centuries. After the fourteenth century, no such fortresses and towers were built, which in turn made it unique in its own way. It was erected to protect the entrance to the gorge from the invasion of the Turks, who used to often fight with the local feudal lords. There were also other fortresses not far away: Sali, Peter's Fortress and Gwirgwin's Fortress, which were located to the northeast.

For a moment I even had the thought of getting to them too, but it was a long way to go, and I still wanted to go to the central park. Which, as it later turned out, is where I would spend the rest of the day.

Still, before heading onward, I decided to take a little break. I nibbled on ripe plums and stared intently at the sky. At one moment in the passing clouds I suddenly saw a huge and drunk Georgian man with a harmonica, with a very dull and loose face. He was playing some bad Georgian song on his harmonica for a long, long time. And his harmonica was already all greasy and shiny, and when one notices it down there, as I do now, it is called a glow of higher harmony.

So I went to the park. It was not very far from the fortress, and the road to it was quite picturesque. Having followed the suspension bridge over the river, bypassing a small square, passing by the market, which was located at the entrance, I could already see its outline and beautiful gates. There were not many tourists that day, and I did not even have to stand in line, as is customary in such parks. Having bought a ticket at the ticket office, I went to see it, anticipating an interesting and exciting walk. Already at the entrance I met a cheerful vendor who was selling exquisite mulled wine and mulled wine. At first he wanted to sell me more drinks, praising his goods, but realizing that I was from St. Petersburg, he poured me a full glass of strong mulled wine and did not even charge me. After exchanging jokes with him, we said goodbye. His drink, by the way, cheered me up and added to my confidence, which came with the bees, who, smelling the tart odor, immediately surrounded me.

Looking at the sculptures and art objects at the entrance, I gradually walked farther and farther away. The park was quite well-maintained and it was noticeable that it was well cared for, clean and comfortable for tourists. Walking along the river, admiring the mountains and various vegetation, after a while I noticed an azure dome, near which people were sitting in a circle, and everyone else went to it with empty bottles. I realized at once that this was the most famous hot spring of mineral water for which this beautiful city was famous.

Passing at a depth of one thousand five hundred meters, rising through wells, the water was saturated with truly healing power. Near the spring there was a woman, a park worker, who kindly poured water into containers that tourists brought with them. Those who did not have them, took a glass and drank as much as they liked. Any traveler, no matter where he came from, could drink and relax here, especially since the atmosphere was very friendly.

The water from the spring was different from that sold in the stores. Here it had a tangible flavor of sulfur and minerals, which did not spoil its taste, but even on the contrary, gave it piquancy and healing properties.

I tried water from both warm and cold springs. Having quenched my thirst and rested a bit, I set off on my way. Without deviating from the chosen route, I continued walking along the Borjomula River, whose water was surprisingly clear and clean. Passing by the covered bridges, breathing in the purest mountain air, I enjoyed the place to the fullest. Following a little deeper still, I saw a waterfall. And I could not pass it by, for the place was truly unique. Not only by the mass of water, which fell in a stormy stream from the steep cliffs, but also by the majestic figure of Prometheus, who held the sacred fire in his hands.

The monument was really unique, I had never seen anything like it anywhere else. And here he appeared for a reason. It is also worth saying a few words about the kinship between Georgia and ancient Greece, because the appearance of Prometheus in these parts was not accidental. Other sculptures that I met in many places testify to the presence of ancient Greeks. First of all in Batumi. The statue of Medea holding a golden fleece in her hands, the gilded statue of Poseidon decorating the fountain, the ensemble "History of Georgia", which I saw earlier in Tbilisi, and others.

And there is nothing surprising in this, because long before the formation of modern Georgia as we know it now, the great and enlightened people of Kolkhi lived in these lands, and Kolkhida, or the Kingdom of Kolkhida, for many centuries was one of the richest and most powerful on this planet. Their power was ensured not only by a favorable geographical location, not only by a developed metallurgical industry, but also by the closest cooperation with ancient Greece, of which to this day we find many examples.

According to legend, somewhere in the Caucasus Mountains Prometheus was chained by Zeus, which the architect of this beautiful monument tried to remind us of.

Carrying fire in his hands, he not only attracted knowledge to the territory of Georgia, but also thousands of tourists who come every year to admire this beautiful monument.

I looked at him mesmerized, not taking my eyes off, realizing in my heart that wherever I directed my gaze, my eyes were fixed on the fire in the hands of Prometheus, in which my life seemed to be burning.

Fully satiated with the place, I went on to explore the park further, going deeper and deeper.

As I leisurely walked along the river, I soon noticed a sign, which indicated that the further path leads me to the sulfur baths. It was possible to pass to them both on foot and by car for a certain fee. I had enough time, so I easily chose the first option, which I did not regret, although the road was not the easiest, with plenty of difficult sections and turns.

Passing by passing cars, I walked leisurely, enjoying the beautiful nature and mountain air. Taking breaks, I stopped at the river bank and took a breather, after which I continued on my way. After half an hour I reached the sulfur baths. After paying a small entrance fee, I decided to stop here for a while, especially since I had been told a lot about their beneficial properties. Sulfur baths are good for the skin, bones, cardiovascular system, they calm the nerves and relax. The water had a distinctive sulfur odor. The temperature was about thirty-six degrees, there were not many people that day, so I allowed myself to relax and rest a little.

After staying there for a little more than half an hour, having gained strength and energy, I went on my way.

At first I thought I would have to go back the same way, but a little later I noticed a path that led somewhere in the mountains. Without thinking long, I decided to follow it. For, as the Chinese proverb says, "if you don't go up the mountain, you won't know the height of the sky".

And it was very good that there were steps, for I had to climb high, and the way was not easy. But I was determined not to turn back and go all the way to the end, no matter what it took, even though while I was climbing I was almost run over by a woman running down the hill. She was American, I realized, and spoke with a distinctive accent that was painfully familiar to me. She was muttering something to herself under her breath, with fear and terror in her eyes, tears on her cheeks, and a scarlet blush on her cheeks. I tried to show her the way, and I hope she understood me. However, she quickly disappeared from my gaze and I continued to climb.

I felt that it took me about forty minutes to climb, and I was sweating profusely, trying not to look down, although I felt that I had climbed high enough. There were no railings, only sparse bushes separating me from the cliff, so I tried to tread very carefully. As I was approaching the very top, I suddenly heard Russian speech. In a moment I noticed a woman of what is called "balzac age", who had not lost her former beauty, and a young man accompanying her. They were actively asking passers-by for directions, which, by the way, were very few, but since no one understood Russian, they could not learn anything. When they saw me, they were immediately happy, and, as they later confessed to me, they could tell from my hat that we spoke the same language. Very quickly we got to talking and found common topics for conversation, and together we began to look for a way out of the park. None of us wanted to go back down, so we just walked forward along the only path that led us farther and farther away. We navigated by markings on the trees, which apparently were left for us by park employees or lost travelers like us. Either way, we were very grateful to them. Carefully making our way through the forest, we soon saw a local who, as best he could, told us to go straight ahead and not to turn around. My companions, by the way, were already visibly nervous and worried, but personally I was confident that we would soon get out. Going deeper and deeper along the path through the forest, we soon found ourselves on the bank of a mountain river, which was not very deep, but there was no bridge or crossing. Even though this caused some doubts and concerns, we had no other option but to take off our shoes and wade across the river. The water was crystal clear and a little cool, but the bottom was not very rocky. Holding on to shrubbery branches and helping each other, we carefully crossed it. After resting on the bank for a bit, we headed further up the trail. After a while, climbing even higher up the mountain, we came to the hermitage of Seraphim of Sarov. This was a holy place to which pilgrims and tourists from all over the country flocked. It was a fully recreated hermitage of the great Russian saint, canonized once by Nicholas II. On the edge of the forest there was his hut where he lived, a well with "holy" water and a stone where, according to legend, he prayed for a thousand days and nights. There was also a church nearby where many people came to pray. I just enjoyed the silence and solitude of this quiet and picturesque place. While my companions performed the necessary rituals and prayed, I looked around and never ceased to be amazed by this place. Having completed all the necessary rituals, we set off on our way. While we were walking, I learned from my companions that they had arrived to Borjomi only yesterday from Kazakhstan. The purpose of their visit, like many tourists, was to take sulfur baths and restore their lost health. They were very polite and talkative people, so it was interesting and exciting to walk with them. Soon we found the right road and did not turn off from it. Passing by the cable car, from which we had a beautiful view of both the park and the city, we decided not to go down it, but to walk to the exit, especially since it was not so long to go. The conversation was fascinating, and soon we saw a path that led us back to the park, where we actually wanted to go. On the way we kept seeing signs that warned us that these forests not only had a variety of flora and fauna, but also had wild animals: bears, roe deer, moose, squirrels and other animals. This did not embarrass me, but it alarmed my companions, who became visibly nervous and wary. However, when we met a group of tourists on the way, they calmed us down, saying that wild animals, especially bears, are very rare here and nobody had seen them in this forest for a long time.

Going lower and lower down the narrow path, we were soon back in the park. In its very center, to the mineral spring with healing water. By this time we were already very tired. It was getting close to sunset, and everyone wanted to rest. We walked a total of at least twenty kilometers, although for me it was a short distance, but for my companions it was a lot. Having quenched our thirst and rested a little, we said goodbye. Wishing each other a happy journey and further adventures, hugging everyone goodbye, I went to the nearest snack bar, for I was very hungry. After eating some kebab, bread and vegetables, drinking some wine, I went home to the place where I was staying. After a final walk along the embankment, the square and the bridge, I went to rest. My legs were very tired by then, so after taking a shower, I spent the evening drinking wine and working on my manuscript. Time passed very quickly, and I didn't even notice that it was midnight. There were so many stars in the sky that I didn't want to leave the terrace, but it was time to go to bed. I had to get up again early in the morning, and there were many more adventures and amazing places waiting for me. When I got to bed, I immediately fell into sleep. Waking up early in the morning, packing my bags, I set off for Khashuri. As I was leaving, I noticed the food in the kitchen that the hostess had carefully prepared for me for breakfast. After saying goodbye and thanking her for the delicious food, I went to the bus station.

10. KHASHURI - SURAMI FORTRESS

I waited for a bus to pass by and went to Khashuri. It was a small town, but the bus was full of people going there. I talked to the woman sitting next to me and while we were traveling she told me an interesting story about this place, which I will now try to recount from memory.

Khashuri settlement has existed since ancient times, but it was first mentioned as a town in the seventeenth century. The town itself and its development is associated with the construction of the Tbilisi - Poti railroad. From 1872 to 1917 this settlement was still called Mikhailovo, then it was called Khashuri, in 1931-34 it was renamed to Stalinisi, then again received its present name.

Since March 1921 during the Sovietization of Georgia there were fierce battles near Khashuri. The Red Army, not without problems and betrayal of Georgian generals, still managed to capture the city and then the Surama Tunnel. After that its active Sovietization continued. And only after the collapse of the Soviet Union it returned to Georgia. The woman also told me that during the Soviet times there were several monuments to Stalin in Khashuri, which were later torn down. One of them, however, was restored in 2000, but then it was torn down again in 2008. Since I was going there for the first time, her story was very interesting for me and helped me to pass a few hours on the way. However, my real goal was not to visit Khashuri, but to visit and go to a nearby village called Surami and visit and see the famous Surami fortress. The Surami fortress was the cornerstone and almost the goal of my entire trip. I think it will be appropriate in this essay to tell the background of my interest in it. After all, I started dreaming about it and the fact that I would someday be able to touch its walls long before my journey. It all started a few years ago, when friends told me about the famous Soviet director Sergei Parajanov, who became famous not only as a director, but also as a painter, sculptor and dissident, who resisted Soviet censorship until the end of his life. His famous films "Shadows of Forgotten Ancestors", "The Color of Pomegranates", "Ashik-Kerib" and especially, I would note, "The Legend of the Surami Fortress" made him famous all over the world. All of them impressed me very much, and each in its own way memorable for its atmosphere, selection of actors and attention to detail. And it was after watching "The Legend of Surami Fortress" that I started to dream of visiting this historical and ancient place. The very history of this fortress, based on an ancient legend, inspired me very much and stirred my imagination. Once it was retold by the Georgian writer Daniel Chonkadze,

and later Parajanov made a wonderful movie based on it. The legend itself says: the people of Georgia, preparing to defend their country from the attack of Muslim invaders, decided to build a fortress, but every time the wall reached the level of the roof, it collapsed. "The wall will stand if the most beautiful young man is walled up in it," said the fortune-teller Vardo. And a young man with blue eyes was found, who made a self-sacrifice to save the Fatherland and the Christian faith. Thanks to this sacrifice, the fortress was erected, and no one and nothing could destroy it anymore. I liked this legend very much, as well as the movie itself, and from that moment I had a dream to visit it. When I arrived at the station, I made a route on the map and found out that from the center of Khashuri to the fortress was about five kilometers on foot. I was feeling great, full of energy and strength, so I decided to walk to it, enjoying the wonderful views of the mountains and local architecture along the way. The path was along a highway, past private houses and ruined factories. The road was very rocky and narrow, it was obviously not the most popular route for tourists, but it didn't bother me. I didn't walk very fast, trying not to hurry anywhere, and after a while I began to feel a sense of hunger creeping up on me. As if with the steadiness of the coming darkness, I began to feel it more and more. And the interesting thing is that just as this thought was born in my head, a ripe plum fell on my head. I looked up and saw several branches of plum trees. The fruit was overripe and was falling on my head under its weight. I took the opportunity to bend the branch closer and picked up pockets full of delicious plums, which helped me a lot on the way, satisfied my hunger and reminded me once again that I had come at a good time.

I was walking along the road on a very narrow path that stretched out and away beyond the horizon. I did not look at the time; it was still morning and there was plenty of time. Eating plums, I kept looking at the fortress, which was located high on the mountain. I walked for about two hours and, despite the heavy backpack on my back, I was not tired at all. Soon I saw the small village of Surami and decided to walk through its narrow streets. I felt a little uneasy because of the dogs that immediately surrounded me and started barking, but I did not get confused, turned to another street and soon they left me alone. I walked a little through the streets of Surami without finding any people or sights, but I noticed a narrow path that went uphill and followed it. The path led straight to the fortress, which I guessed at once. I climbed the stony path carefully, and after a while I came to a hill on which the fortress itself was perched on a high rock. The sight before me was incredible. I could not believe that I had finally reached it and was standing in front of it. The highest walls and the square tower immediately attracted my eyes and stunned me with its majestic and powerful appearance. The Georgian flag was flying on the tower itself, and it looked like on a postcard that I had once had in my childhood. I remembered it immediately, but I have long forgotten how I got it, but this view and the main tower and the flag were remembered for life. It was all the more amazing that now I could see the fortress with my own eyes, standing next to the wall. Admiring its thick walls, I was about to explore it when I noticed an old woman, who looked to be at least a hundred years old, sitting on a ruined bench near the fortress and looking at me intently. I immediately said hello to her, and she nodded and gave me a curious look. I thought to myself that my grandmother must know a lot of interesting stories about both the fortress and Surami, so I decided that I would ask her about it as soon as I finished my tour. As I climbed higher and higher up the walls of the fortress, I noticed a narrow staircase that led to the fortress itself. I decided to follow it, even though the railing of the stairs was wobbling and going in different directions. I carefully climbed the stairs and found myself inside the fortress, or what was left of it.

Once standing on steep cliffs, it consisted of two parts - the lower and the upper. As I began to look around, I came to the conclusion that only the upper part had been preserved. The fortress walls here are multi-layered, up to three and a half meters thick, which testified to the life that went on inside it century after century. If the walls were partially destroyed as a result of enemy raids, they were built again, it was visible to the naked eye, as it was unacceptable to leave the strategically important place of Georgia without protection. According to the layers of the fortress wall, I tried to determine the order in which the individual elements of the fortress were erected. In the beginning there was only a tower and a fence, only the tower has survived to this day. I did not know exactly how many floors the tower had, but its height was more than ten meters. Inside the fortress walls I immediately saw the ruins of various buildings: a citadel, a palace and a church. The courtyard of the citadel is at a level of several meters, and its wall was crowned with teeth and looked like the walls that were erected in the eighteenth century. Here I noticed many single and double loopholes. The church consisted of two parts covered with one roof - I had never seen such church architecture anywhere else in Georgia, and I was immediately struck by it. The church had two entrances and an annex with an area of two by three meters, which served as a tomb. Inside on the walls of the church you could see many frescoes and icons, which were left by pilgrims and believers who visited these lands at different times. Also on the territory of the fortress are the remains of the palace, which are covered with earth. The palace was enclosed by a fence about two meters high and about eight meters long. As I later learned, the major restoration of the fortress took place at the end of the sixteenth and beginning of the seventeenth centuries, as the remains of the walls erected during this period are best preserved. The only entrance to the fortress is in the northern wall. The fortress of Surami has at all times been considered very strong, having withstood the sieges of many enemies, though the sieges of time it has unfortunately not been able to withstand. I thought about all this while I was inside, looking at the ruins of the walls, enjoying the beautiful view of the mountains and the nearby villages below. While I was contemplating further plans, it began to rain. The timid first drops heralded a further downpour, which, according to the forecast, was about to begin. I figured that it would be very muddy here soon enough, and the stairs would be very slippery. So I decided to head back before it was too late. As I carefully left the fortress, I noticed again the old woman, who was still sitting there, staring at me intently; she did not seem to be frightened by the rain. It didn't frighten me either, so I decided to talk to her a little and ask her about the area.

When I approached her, I introduced myself and briefly told her my story and how I came to be here. She was a little surprised, but she did not ask any questions. Her name was Gulisvardi and she was ninety-three years old. She lived nearby and looked after the fortress, feeding the rare dogs that wandered around.

Surprisingly, she had a good memory, and she answered my questions about Surami and the fortress quite clearly. Gulisvardi told me that Surami had been on an important caravan route for centuries and had been inhabited for a long time. Perhaps it was what Pliny the Elder meant by Surium when he wrote about these parts. But the city itself appeared in history only in the twelfth century. And almost immediately the golden era of its history began - it became the residence of the Eristavs of Kartli, who received the title of Surameli. Surami remained the capital of the region throughout the thirteenth century, but after the coming of the Mongols it gradually lost its importance, and the Surami eristavs themselves disappeared somewhere. For a long time it remained just a small town. In the spring of 1614 Shah Abbas during his first campaign to Georgia came to these places and, according to legend, built a fortress in Surami. It is possible that the present-day Surami Castle was built at that time, but it is not known. By the middle of the eighteenth century the town belonged to Prince Givi Amilakhvari, who fought with Iranians and Georgian kings. In 1744 he was defeated near Anchabeti (near Tskhinvali), after which the Tsar's army approached Surami and Amilakhvari surrendered. Surami fortress was destroyed. But 20 years later the Russian army came and rebuilt it in order to have a base for the war with the Turks. From the beginning of the nineteenth century there was a climatic resort here. During the Soviet era, local residents were actively distributed to dachas in the local area, so since then Surami has resembled a dacha village. Only the fortress reminds of the beautiful and great times. Having written down her last words in my notebook, I looked at the square tower for the last time with an elusive sadness, thanked and said goodbye to Gulisvardi and headed back. I had originally wanted to spend the night in Surami and even decided to chat with passers-by at the bus stop about whether I should. But they told me that there was nothing to see except the fortress, and before the weather turned bad, I'd better move on. So after having lunch at a local eatery, I went to the bus station to go to Gori, the next point on my journey.

11. GORI

We didn't have to wait long for transportation. Not even an hour later, the bus pulled up. As was my habit, I sat on the back seat near the window and opened a book. Finally I had time to read a little, relax and enjoy the beautiful view from the window. To be honest, I always look forward to moments like this and often anticipate them. I have never traveled by motor vehicle as often as I have this summer and fall, so I always remember with a touch of sadness and pleasure these wonderful moments of my life when you can just stare out the window, listening to pleasant music, and reflect on the place you've traveled to. While we were waiting for all the passengers, I had time to read a little about the city of Gori and its surroundings, because until now the only thing I had heard about it was that it was the birthplace of Joseph Stalin. His personality is so controversial that I will not tell much about him here. Anyone who reads this book will probably know all about him very well. However, I wanted to know much more about the place I went to, and soon enough, reading dry text from Wikipedia was not enough for me, so I decided to ask my neighbors. After a while, I noticed that the bus had filled up with passengers and we set off. An elderly man sat down next to me, with whom I decided to have a little chat. To my surprise, he turned out to be quite friendly and talkative, which I immediately liked. His name was Zurab. As he soon told me, he was on his way to visit his son, who lived in Gori. He also inquired about the purpose of my trip. I decided to tell him briefly about the amazing places I had been fortunate enough to visit in the last few days. As my story progressed, I noticed a genuine interest and surprise on his face, which I was certainly flattered by. After he had listened to me, I suggested that he add to my story and tell me about the place where he was born. After all, he was born and grew up in Gori, and, as I soon realized, knew this city quite well.

From his story I realized that Gori is one of the oldest cities in Georgia. Its history began in the distant seventh century AD. The city took its name from the rock formation (goraki) in the center of the city, where the remains of the ancient fortress, which is now called Goritsikhe, are located. However, when Zurab was studying at school, they were told that the foundation of the city may well be connected with the name of David IV the Builder, who lived on this land much earlier. King David was a man of war. He built an Armenian city in Georgia, established many churches and monasteries and named this city Gura (Gori). In the last few years, many archaeological excavations have been conducted in the city, with the help of which it was found out that there were urban-type settlements in the place of Gori long before the beginning of our era. Moreover, there are stories that in 1946 a landslide near the northern wall of Goritsikhe exposed a layer of ancient times. A lot of pottery and amazing artifacts were also discovered, which tells us that people with rich knowledge and crafts lived here from time immemorial. And since then Gori has passed from hand to hand of Georgian, Armenian, Iranian, Iranian, Ottoman, Persian and Russian kings. Each of them left behind a piece of the culture to which he belonged. Also an important date in the history of the city was 1920, when the largest earthquake in those parts of the country occurred, which destroyed most of the city. Zurab's grandmother said that the earthquake started in the morning. The first tremor destroyed the water tower.

Within ten minutes, hundreds of buildings collapsed. Clouds of dust, pink from the sun, stood over the city. The street was littered with smoking rubble. Women sobbed and dogs barked.... At this point his story was interrupted, the bus stopped, and I realized that we had arrived. Saying goodbye to Zurab, I took my bag and got out. It was about four o'clock in the afternoon, the weather was beautifully sunny, the sun was blazing hot and there was a light breeze, which made it very comfortable to be in this place.

I had enough energy, so I immediately went for a walk around the old city. Walking along its streets, it immediately caught my eye that practically all the buildings had been qualitatively restored and looked a bit artificial. There was not that natural shabbiness, inherent in other Georgian cities. Not that this fact upset me, but it was a bit surprising. I liked the architecture and the layout of the houses very much. I especially liked the beautiful wrought iron balconies, which looked simply gorgeous. There were very few tourists, which I also noticed at once. Walking along the narrow streets between the houses, I could already see the fortress of Goritsikhe, which is located on a high hill and was clearly visible. However, I decided to postpone my visit a bit and first get to my hotel to leave my things and take a shower. Especially since, according to the map, my hotel was a half hour walk away, which was the perfect opportunity for me to take a good look at everything along the way and walk around. So I did. My hotel was called Guest House Svetlana. I rang the bell and was immediately opened by the hostess, a not young but very friendly and welcoming woman, who showed me to my room, the sitting area and the bathroom. Having rested a bit, I took a shower and had lunch. The hostess's name was Svetlana, and before going for a walk around the city, I decided to have a little chat with her. She spoke excellent Russian and, as she said, she often had Russian-speaking visitors staying with her and never had any problems with them. Svetlana also told me about all the sights I should visit, showed me where the bazaar was if I wanted to buy souvenirs, told me about museums and restaurants where I could always have a great dinner. Thanking her for her advice, I paid and went straight to the fortress, which I was already so eager to see and examine in great detail. Already on the approach to the fortress I noticed rare tourists, who for some reason did not immediately go up to the fortress walls, and decided to go around it a little. I decided to follow them and had no regrets. Right next to the fortress there was a monument to the Fallen Heroes or Memorial to the Defenders of Goritsikhe. Eight huge warriors with serious and a bit creepy faces were sitting at an invisible round table, and each of them was missing a part of his body: an arm, a leg, a head. As I guessed later, it was to remind people that no battle is without casualties, and even the bravest warriors pay for their fearlessness and desire to protect their native lands with a piece of

themselves. Nearby was a plaque with a description, from which I learned that the monument was installed in 2008 and since that time has attracted a lot of attention to both the city itself and the fortress. After taking a good look at each warrior, I decided to go up to the fortress walls. The tourists I had seen earlier also decided to go up, and among them was a guide who was telling the history of the fortress and its peculiarities. From him I learned that Goritsikhe is located on a high cliff at the confluence of the rivers Liakhva and Kura. The Kura was the route from Europe to Asia, and the Liakhva was the route from the north to Transcaucasia, and the fortress allowed to control these routes. It was erected in the thirteenth century. The citadel was built in the shape of an ellipse and had high and strong stone walls. The western part, called Tskhra-Kara or "Nine Gates", is particularly famous. The fortress was fortified with several rows of walls and had a secret tunnel leading to the nearest water source. Already in the V-IV centuries B.C., there were fortifications on this place, performing the function of a prison, as historical sources testify.

In the Middle Ages Goritsikhe was the subject of conflicts between Persians, Ottomans and Georgians, often changing its owners. Since its construction, it has been subjected to numerous restorations. At the end of XVIII - beginning of XIX centuries the fortress passed into the hands of the Russian army, but over time it lost its defensive function and began to deteriorate, which, however, did not prevent it from entering the list of cultural monuments of national importance in Georgia.

It is not difficult to get into the fortress. It is more convenient to do it from the side of the cathedral. Going around the hill clockwise, I together with a group of tourists went up the path that led to the South Gate. The gate was a brick tower with a Persian style arch. Going beyond the gate, we came to a flat clearing from which the whole city was perfectly visible. All the buildings and structures were very well visible. I especially remembered the modern building of the House of Justice and the soccer stadium.

Meanwhile, our guide continued his story and told us that once there was a temple in the fortress, but later it disappeared at an unknown time. Rumor has it that it collapsed in 1920. Now only the western wall is left of it, which practically merges with the fortress wall. Where everything else stood, you can now see the remains of an ancient structure that looks more like a bunker. It should be assumed that during the construction of this bunker in Soviet times all the remains of the temple were destroyed.

That was the end of our guide's story, everyone went away and continued exploring the walls of the fortress.

I decided to make a small break and rest a little. I sat on the most picturesque place near the wall and for about half an hour contemplated the city and the surrounding mountains.

As I looked around, I noticed a large, dense bush on the slope and decided to focus on it. But not on the leaves themselves, but on their shadows.

At first I started to contemplate the shadows of the leaves on one branch and gradually moved on to contemplating the whole bush, not letting my eyes return to their usual mode.

Perhaps it was my fatigue or nervous excitement, but I became so absorbed in the contemplation of shadows that I could form the shadows into visually perceptible arrays as freely as leaves are usually formed into arrays. The effect was startling. I decided to narrow my eyes a little so that the shadows seemed to layer on top of each other, merging into one. It had incredible depth and even a kind of transparency. I could clearly distinguish every dot, every crack and grain of sand in the place I was looking at. And there was a shadow over it all, like a superfine, indescribably transparent film.

For a while I even fell out of reality, completely immersed in contemplation, I forgot about everything in the world. The inner dialog in my head was stopped, and for a moment it even seemed to me that together with it the world also stopped. It was amazing. After sitting like that for about an hour, I completely rested and regained my strength.

I got up and started to descend. On the way I already realized that I wanted to go to the Stalin Museum and take a good look at everything there.

The Joseph Stalin Museum is impossible to miss. The building stands on the only green area in the city center near the fortress, called Stalin Square. The main wide street, Stalin Avenue of course, leads to the square. His monument is located in front of the museum.

Having paid ten GEL for the entrance, I decided to visit it. As I entered the main hall, I was immediately told that the museum was a tribute to a great countryman and nothing more. In front of the entrance there was a large plaque on the wall, from which I learned that the museum was founded in 1957 and has been in the same place ever since. However, earlier, in 1937, a memorial room had been arranged in Stalin's house in honor of the still living leader.

The two-story building, which houses the museum's exposition, was designed by the Georgian architect Archil Kudiani. In front of the building there is a monument to Stalin - the creation of Silovan Kakabadze and a saloon car in which the leader traveled to conferences in Yalta and Tehran. In front of the entrance to the building there is also a copy of the former house of the dictator. The poor room where Dzhugashvili spent the first years of his life was covered by a structure that gave it the character of a mausoleum. The exposition in the main building is permanent, and the more than forty thousand exhibits collected are distributed in six thematic halls: "Koba's activities before and during the October Revolution"; "The period 1925-1939, when "Dzhugashvili's party fought for the economic and cultural development of the country"; "Photographs from the period of World War II and the conferences in Tehran, Yalta and Potsdam"; "One of Dzhugashvili's posthumous masks"; "Gifts to the Ghoul"; "Comrade K's office with personal belongings". I went to the first floor. The stairs leading there were covered with a red carpet, and at the top stood another statue of the leader. As I walked further and further in, I caught myself thinking that I was in a socialist reservation, and the interior with red marble on the walls matched that feeling perfectly.

I also noticed a lot of paintings, woven rugs, and all kinds of other art on the walls. My eye was caught by the exhibit "The Early Life of Ghoul", which showed the dictator as a diligent student and role model for the youth. In most paintings of those years, Koba is the only one posing with a book. Information about the conferences in Tehran, Yalta and Potsdam presented the dictator as the main player, almost single-handedly deciding the fate of the world. And in this, unfortunately, there was some truth. After that I decided to examine the gifts that the commander-in-chief had received from the brotherly nations. Among them were: a bas-relief from Lebanese cider with the image of Koba, a portrait from colored sand from Ukraine, a Romanian composition from tobacco leaves - with Joseph Dzhugashvili in the main role. Poles made a commemorative plaque with the slogan "Stalin - peace and freedom between peoples". There were also Georgian vases, an Iranian carpet, an Italian set of pipes and Chinese porcelain among the exhibits. This part of the exhibition is one of the most interesting - the works were often made with extraordinary skill and therefore quite spectacular.

The interiors of his study, on the other hand, were very ascetic, unlike my perceptions, which varied slightly.

The chief's personal belongings such as cigarettes, ceremonial uniforms and a telephone were also placed in his study.

At this point I decided to end my inspection and leave the premises, for in the back of my mind I was already getting creeped out by the place.

Leaving the museum, I immediately noticed the carriage in which Dzhugashvili traveled to participate in conferences in Tehran, Yalta and Potsdam.

Taking the opportunity, I decided to look in it too.

The car was manufactured in St. Petersburg and originally served as a service car of the tsarist government. Later it was adapted to Koba Ivanovich's needs and became the temporary home and office of the Soviet dictator.

For security reasons, it was heavily armored and the windows were replaced with bulletproof windows. The weight of the car increased to 83 tons - twice as much as a standard car of this design. The interior was decorated comfortably, but without excessive pomp. The walls inside are lined with mahogany. The room is divided into a conference area with a large table, a kitchen, a toilet with a bath, a bedroom and a technical area.

Speaking in general, visiting the museum and the wagon in which this bloody ghoul traveled was quite a rewarding experience for me. I learned a lot of new things that I had no idea about and saw a lot of interesting paintings and artwork.

Meanwhile, the time was getting close to dusk, and I decided to walk around the city some more before going to bed along the main streets.

Walking along Tsereteli Street, I turned first to Rustaveli Street, then to February 25th Street, and then to Dzhugashvili Street. All of them are not pedestrianized, but the paving stones laid down slowed down the traffic a lot and allowed me not to fear cars. In the old town of Gori I noticed two churches, one of which was just under construction. The second was the Church of the Virgin Mary, and it was in beautiful condition. Inside was bustling with life and I noticed a lot of nuns going out and coming back in, it was interesting but I didn't bother to find out the reason and went on my way. Coming out of the old town, I found myself on Chavchavadze Avenue. In the center there was a tiny park of Nikoloz Baratashvili with a full-length monument to him.

I decided to have some rest near it. Passing by a row of benches, I noticed an elderly man feeding pigeons. I decided to sit next to him, opened a book, wanted to read a little, but at that moment the man sitting next to me was distracted by me and decided to talk to me. He was very surprised by the very fact of having a book in my hands. As he said at once, young people nowadays almost do not read books, and this fact saddens him very much. Taking the opportunity, I decided to ask him about the personality and fate of the poet, near the monument to whom we were sitting.

The man answered with marked enthusiasm and immediately began his story.

From his words I learned that Nikoloz Baratashvili was born in 1817 in Tiflis in the family of Prince Meliton Baratashvili and Princess Efimia Orbeliani. His family, despite the princely origin, was not rich and noble, but the poor material situation was more than compensated by spiritual wealth. Among the ancestors of the poet were brilliant military figures, poets and even Catholicos-Patriarch of Georgia.

The true portrait of Nikoloz Baratashvili has not survived, contemporaries described him as a skinny young man with brown hair wearing a cherkeska or a small Georgian cap, cheerful, active, with a lively temper, sharp on the tongue. From his youth the poet limped on one leg. According to legend, he had an unfortunate fall down the stairs and remained lame forever. It was this injury that prevented him from joining the army, although he always dreamed of a military career. Young Baratashvili also dreamed of studying at a Russian university, but his father's poverty did not allow this dream to come true, it closed the road to social status.

Even during his studies he was imbued with the ideas of humanism and national freedom, which were later reflected in his work. In the 1840s, he headed a literary circle, even then he had the fame of a poet.

One of the most important themes of his work was his unrequited love for Princess Ekaterina Alexandrovna Chavchavadze, sister of Nina Alexandrovna, Griboyedov's widow, infamous as "the black rose of Tiflis". Ekaterina married Prince Dadiani, heir to the throne of Mingrelia; Nikoloz Baratashvili - poor, lame - had no chance. And yet the poems dedicated to Ekaterina Alexandrovna became a model of brilliant love lyrics. During his lifetime, Baratashvili did not publish a single work. In 1844 he was forced to enter the civil service in Ganja. A year later the poet contracted malaria and died suddenly. None of his relatives could come to the burial. At the time of his death he was twenty-seven years old.

And only a few years later Baratashvili's beloved, the same princess Ekaterina Alexandrovna, gave a notebook with poems dedicated to her to another Georgian poet - Ilya Chavchavadze. The latter published several works, and 16 years after his death his collection of poems was published. This is how Georgia got a great poet. At the end of his story the man gave me a small book of his poems, to which I was surprised and thanked him for a long time. It was a wonderful gift for me, which pleases me to this day.

All the following days, being in Georgia, I read his poems and never ceased to marvel, it was a truly wonderful discovery for me.

Meanwhile, the sun had almost set and it was getting darker and darker, so I thanked my interlocutor and went to my hotel. On the way, I bought a bottle of wine at a local store to work on my notes some more.

When I got to the hotel, I noticed that I had a roommate in the room where I was seated. An elderly American who unfortunately was not a very talkative or friendly person, so we didn't get to socialize, which didn't upset me too much. I worked on my manuscript for a few more hours, finished my wine and fell asleep.

When I woke up early in the morning, I received a message from my friends, who asked me how I was doing and informed me that tomorrow there would be another beautiful concert in Batumi, which I should definitely attend. I was very excited and happy about this prospect, so I decided to return to Batumi for a day.

I informed Svetlana about my plans, said goodbye cordially and went to the bus station. I had bought an early bus ticket in advance, and I had just a few hours to walk around old Gori once again and enjoy its architecture. As I passed by Goritsikhe, its history once again ran through my mind.

Now, when enough time has passed, I often remember it.

I arrived at the bus station an hour before my departure, so I had time to have breakfast and not to hurry anywhere. So I did. The ride was about six hours long, so I replenished my provisions and, when the bus pulled up, sat in my favorite seat in the back of the cabin. Once the bus was filled with passengers, we were off. Already in the first minutes of the journey I realized that I had not slept at all, so I was very sleepy. I put the book aside and fell asleep. When I woke up, I could already see from the window that we were somewhere near, and the trip, which could have been tedious, had flown by, I had time to rest and regain my strength.

12. BATUMI - END OF THE TRIP

The weather was beautiful in Batumi. The sun was shining, the sea was shimmering blue, and tankers and barges with goods were still standing on the horizon waiting for unloading.

After throwing my backpack behind me and paying the driver, I immediately went for a walk around my favorite places, getting closer to my hotel, which was next to Europe Square. There seemed to be even more tourists, and the streets were very crowded that evening. When I arrived at the hotel I saw the same company and the same guests, which surprised me a little, for I thought the tourists changed much more frequently. After paying for a couple of nights, recharging my batteries and leaving my things, I went to Giggles. My friends were already waiting for me there. That evening Anton Ripatti and Astemir Marshenkulov were performing with a very interesting program.

Coming to the club, I was once again surprised by the hospitality and kindness of its owners. All comers were treated with tasty soup and drinks, dogs were still happily running around in the hope that they would be fed, and spectators were still smoking and chatting carefree with each other while waiting for the concert.

My friends arrived at the very beginning, which made me very happy and excited. Meanwhile the concert started, and we spent the next hour and a half in a psychedelic-meditative atmosphere accompanied by instrumental kraut-poloten.

The concert flowed smoothly into the performance, and with each song it became more interesting. There were a lot of light bulbs, colorful lights and psychedelic musical sketches. So I really enjoyed the experience and, as is often the case with me, I was very surprised.

I often lower my expectations before concerts in order to have a more colorful and intense experience. This tactic has never failed me, and this time the concert exceeded all my expectations.

It ended late at night, we still had a little time with friends to walk along the night promenade and share news and impressions.

My friends asked me a lot about my adventures and were surprised by my acquaintances and stories along the way. It seemed inconceivable for them to walk so much in the hope of seeing the Suram fortress or climbing the mountain in Borjomi park, and many other discoveries of mine aroused keen interest. The rest of the day passed, we said goodbye warmly and went to bed.

When I woke up the next day, I realized that this was my last day in Georgia and I had to spend it as relaxed and enjoyable as possible.

Therefore, from the very morning, after a dense and delicious breakfast, I went for a long walk to the part of the city where I had not been yet, reaching almost to the airport. Along the way, I found many more sights and interesting places that I tried to keep in my mind and keep in my memories. Reading poetry during moments of rest in the parks, I remembered the past days and all the people I had met during that week. Already close to dinner it became so hot that I decided not to waste time and go to the sea to enjoy bathing in the beautiful emerald water of the Black Sea, which was already beckoning me and calling me to its salty bosom.

Having chosen the most deserted and picturesque place, I settled down by the water and spent the rest of the day swimming and sunbathing in the scorching sun. Gradually, there were more and more people on the beach, the music was getting louder and louder from the beachside cafes, and time was flying by at an increasing speed. For a while I even fell asleep, but quickly woke up and continued swimming. Moreover, the water was very warm, so it was a great pleasure to be in it. Already in the water I began to notice the first reflections of a beautiful pink-peach sunset, which was so beautiful and picturesque that all the eyes of tourists were directed at it. People just stood in amazement at this marvelous picture and seemed unable to believe their eyes. I myself was simply amazed by this sight and could not leave the beach until the sun finally disappeared behind the horizon. As soon as the first lights came on, I realized that I was already very hungry, so I decided to have something to eat.

After a small dinner, I walked around the night city for a few more hours, enjoying the beautiful night illumination, music and performances of artists on the promenade, which are very numerous every night in these hot nights. All of them were from different countries and created a very motley and rich color of folk and original creativity, which certainly decorated this wonderful promenade that has long been a meeting point for travelers and tourists from all over the world.

I walked until late at night and only by midnight I remembered that I had an early morning bus and my legs were so tired that they needed an urgent rest. When I reached my hotel, I decided to drink tea before going to bed and contemplate the stars for the last time. Walking to the patio, I sat down in a picturesque spot and began to look at the constellations. There weren't many stars in the sky, but those that were there were shining very brightly that night. I was so engrossed in the act of contemplation that I didn't even notice the young man sitting next to me, who was curious about me. Perhaps he just could not sleep, or he was depressed by loneliness, or he was simply interested in keeping me company. He immediately offered me a cigarette and introduced himself. His name was Mikhail, and he lived across the street. Literally immediately we began to talk like old friends. He obviously wanted to talk and tell his story, the unpleasant moments of which he kept carefully hushed up. As it turned out, he was a former businessman who had long ago retired from business, went on a well-deserved vacation, bought a house and settled in a beautiful place. His life was clearly a success. He enjoyed it, but there were also some unpleasant moments in politics and culture that bothered him a lot, so he discussed them with fervor, cursing the government and the world's elites who had prevented him from becoming a truly "big man" in his youth. However, I never understood what he meant by that, I think his life was already successful and he lives in a great place, but apparently he wanted more. He also asked about my adventures, experiences and hobbies with interest, which made him noticeably curious, trying to comment and give advice on places that were out of my sight. Listening to his comments, I was already well aware of how much remained unexplored and amazing in this wonderful country, to which I will definitely return. But in the meantime we continued to communicate on a variety of topics. About politics, art, music, Bartashvili's poems, the past and the near future. Once again I met a wonderful and intelligent interlocutor, which I rarely meet in R., which makes me sad, but also motivates me to return to this wonderful land where life is blooming in all its splendor.

We ended up talking with Michael for about two more hours, which flew by. He wanted to invite me to the wedding of his grandson, which was to take place tomorrow, but when he learned that I was leaving in the morning, he was obviously a little upset and expressed regret. But he left me his contacts and advised me to find him the next time I was in Batumi. We said goodbye warmly and I went to bed, falling into a deep sleep the moment my head touched the pillow.

13. FAREWELL TO BATUMI - THE WAY BACK

The next day, waking up early in the morning, I went to the bus station. Everyone in the hotel was still asleep. I packed my things carefully, so as not to wake anyone up, and left. The weather was fine, there was a light breeze from the sea, the streets were still deserted, and the small stores and stores were just starting to open.

On my way out, I stopped at the market to buy water and supplies I would need for the trip. Having bought everything I needed, I decided to walk around the quiet streets a little longer and enjoy for the last time this year the beautiful view of the Black Sea, on whose beaches I had sunbathed yesterday.

I sat down on the shore and contemplated the water. And the first thing I noticed was that the sea at dawn is special, usually much calmer than during the day. In the morning it can be mirror-like. I have never seen such a thing in the daytime. Also, there was no one on the beach at this time, which I certainly liked. At such moments you have a feeling that the sea is only yours, it belongs only to you and no one else. And even if it was only for a few minutes, I felt it clearly. There were no people, no ice cream sellers, no children's laughter, no boats, no jet skis. And only very quietly you hear the sound of the waves and the faint cry of seagulls somewhere in the distance. At such moments the so-called "unity with nature", which so often happens in ordinary life, takes place. I enjoyed every minute, but also watched the time, for soon I was to leave this beautiful place.

After a while I went to the bus station. Especially since it was very close by. On the way I stopped by the local market to buy supplies for the road. Surprisingly, it was already crowded in the morning, so I had to push around a bit, and I didn't find the right vendor right away, but I bought everything I needed with the last money I had and went to wait for my bus. I sat down on the steps of the local church, or rather, it was a Catholic church built in the late nineties that looked quite modern, and waited. As I waited, all the people I'd met and places I'd been lucky enough to visit flashed through my mind. It was a session of nostalgia and pleasant memories that reverberated in my soul with a little sadness and at the same time gave me hope for my imminent return. I don't know if it will be in a year or two, but I didn't want to leave. At the same time I was well aware that I was expected at work, and things would not do themselves. While I was thinking and reminiscing, my bus arrived and the first passengers were getting ready to board. I sat at the end of the cabin and stared out the window, trying to memorize every tree and building in the area, trying to remember every detail.

Contemplation had always been one of my favorite pastimes, and I indulged in it quite often and at the first opportunity. And now, on this gray and a little sad morning, I was looking at the facades of the buildings, the faces of the people and the surrounding landscape, on which a small trace of sadness for the past days seemed to fall like a shadow. And yet it was a pleasant sadness, which always comes to me at such moments. The bus filled up and we set off. While we were traveling, I caught myself thinking that time flows much faster when you go back. This fact set me on a whole chain of thoughts, and I decided to look into this phenomenon more thoroughly. I realized that for such complex beings, we are too bad at estimating time. Especially in the short term - seconds, minutes, hours. My estimation depended on subjective factors, my mood and what I was doing. This subjectivity led me to some very strange phenomena, including one where the road back seems shorter and time flows faster. I even remembered that there's a whole concept in English called the return trip effect, which can be translated into Russian as the return trip effect. When we go to an unfamiliar place and then come back from there, it seems to us that the way back takes much less time, even though we have traveled the same distance.

When I started to recall all sorts of studies on this subject, I thought that this effect might be related to storytelling - the way information is conveyed through experience and memory. The essence of it was that the backtracking effect could only occur if I knew I was going backwards.

In my opinion, this effect occurs for two reasons:

1. Driving to my destination, I thought I was running late, and so I paid much more attention to time. When I was driving back, this did not happen.

2. Driving back, I saw places I already knew. Because of this, I felt more comfortable and time moved faster.

I also concluded that I was too optimistic about the road, and because of that it took much longer. However, when I drove back, I was slightly overestimating my expectations, and so it seemed to me that the journey took less time.

The backtracking effect could have occurred for each of these reasons separately or for a combination of them. But my senses did not deceive me, and I experienced time differently, regardless of logic and clocks.

Time flew by, the scenery outside the window was changing rapidly, and already in the evening we arrived in Tbilisi to take a short break, change the driver, have a snack and a little walk.

I did not go far away from the bus and walked a little in a small square near the road. Along the way, exchanging impressions with passengers who, just like me, were all on their way back to RF.

Not even half an hour later, we set off again with a new driver, who turned out to be a bit friendlier than the previous one, which immediately caught my eye.

Time flew, and by midnight we were already at the border, which, by the way, we passed much faster, and nobody had any problems with documents this time.

By morning we were back in Stavropol, where, unfortunately, the weather was very bad. It was dense fog, pouring rain and noticeably cool. By that time it was already deep fall outside, and there was no trace of the sunny atmosphere we had in Georgia. So I didn't even want to walk around the streets so as not to spoil the impression. I had breakfast in a local cafe and went to the airport. I already had a plane to St. Petersburg in the afternoon, and my adventure was rapidly coming to an end.

The wait for the flight was thankfully not long, and the time flew by quickly enough. After settling into my seat, I flew back.

When the plane arrived in St. Petersburg, it was already dark, and it was raining so familiarly and habitually that for a moment I felt even sadder.

Stepping off the plane, I stood on the edge of the rubbed iron steps of the gangway and looked into the darkness. It was endless and silent. Out of it came a cool, wet wind, full of many unfamiliar odors and human voices.

As I descended to the ground, I stepped a few meters aside and looked at the plane, which was like a huge iron bird that fascinated and mesmerized me at the same time.

From the side, the airplane really looked like a bird shining with electric lights, flying, in my mind, to an unknown destination. I looked at the point where the tail was visible, and then at the cockpit - nothing but dark emptiness was visible on either side.

I turned and walked away. I didn't think much about where I was going, but soon the asphalt road and the airport terminal were beneath my feet. The noise of the turbines behind me gradually faded, and soon I could hear things I hadn't listened to before: the squeak of my sneakers, the sound of the wind, and the quiet sound of my own footsteps.

About the Author

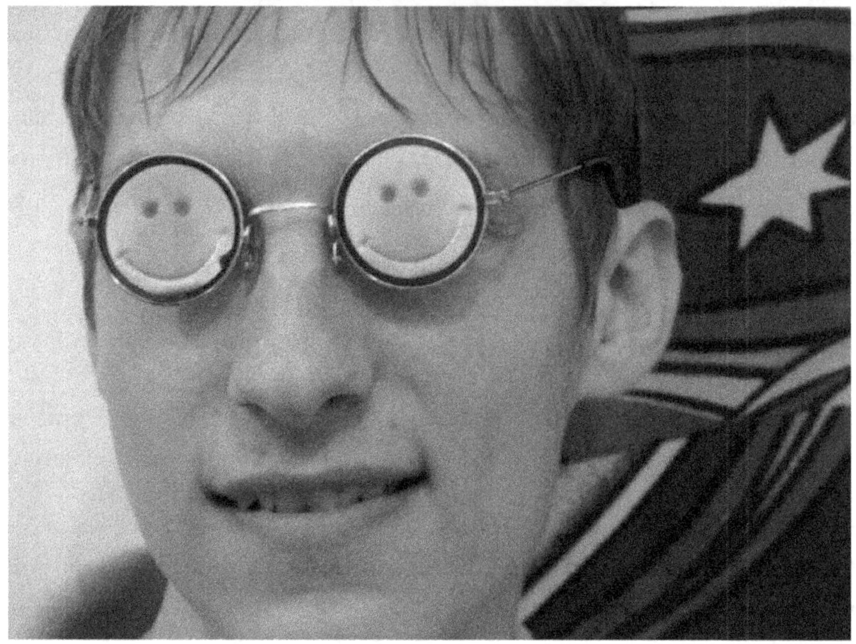

Ilya Tsarev is a Russian artist, writer and musician. In his work he uses the pseudonym acidether.

Ilya Tsarev was born on March 14, 1987 in Omsk, in the family of Tatiana and Sergey Tsarev. Since childhood he was a versatile child, was engaged in various sports: swimming, soccer, tennis, where he achieved certain successes, received awards and sports discharges.

After studying at school he entered Omsk Aviation College named after N.E. Zhukovsky, specializing in "automatic control systems" (ACS), after which he entered the Faculty of Philosophy and Cultural Studies "Omsk State Pedagogical University".

Despite the predilection for the humanities, in the first years of independent life had to work in technical specialties, first as an adjuster at the plant OmPO "Irtysh", then in the field of telecommunications and telephone marketing. However, the craving for self-education saturated the inquisitive mind with new ideas and discoveries, and at the end of 2010 Ilya moved to St. Petersburg for more impressive earnings and self-realization, where in time and settled his creative laboratory. He began to try his hand at prose, during a short trip to Smolensk he wrote his first book "Lessons of Freedom" in co-authorship with Vladimir Kolontsov, which was published the same year. At the same time, Ilya expands his creative pursuits, becoming fascinated by the philosophy of anti-natalism, Dadaism, avant-garde, surrealism, industrial, marginal poetry and prose, collecting his musical collection of "strange records". However, despite his love for art, he had to try himself in different roles, having changed many jobs and specialties: sales manager, furniture assembler, technician, adjuster, telemarketer, assistant bankruptcy trustee, etc. Currently works in a law firm.

Prose and literary experiences

From an early age, Ilya loved to read, especially this hobby captured him after moving to St. Petersburg, where he actively began to communicate and get acquainted with artists, theater artists, musicians, scientists and writers. All this led to a variety of subjects and ideas that he wanted to realize and share with others. Above all with his friends. He begins to write his first essays, poems and stories.

Not satisfied with the small form of his works he moves for a while to Smolensk to visit his friend Vladimir Kolontsov, where he co-authors his first book "Lessons of Freedom". Having finished this work he moves back to St. Petersburg, where he continues to write stories and novels, occasionally participating in literary competitions. For a long time, in his spare time, he writes an autobiographical novel "Josef". The novel was quite "raw", "immature and not worthwhile", although it demonstrates the author's extensive encyclopedic erudition in matters of literature, philosophy and music. It is available for reading on social networks and thematic literary sites.

Having finished this work, Ilya does not stop and continues to write. One after another stories come out: Gorge, Hike, in the shadow and others.

Over time, Ilya becomes more and more fond of poetry and writes a large poem called "The Land of the Stupid", which was later included in a collection of works with the same name. It is published in 2022 in a small edition.

Art Brut and Outsider Art

Since 2016, Ilya has been painting. In the same year he creates his first paintings, which refer to the versatility and versatility of his creativity. In his art, Ilya is not afraid of experimentation, quotability and echoes with iconic outsider artists, in connection with which he often creates a discussion field around his works. He draws passionately, creating increasingly complex and detailed works, while not hiding the fact that he has no superficial understanding of art brut and outsider art, but in his artworks he exclusively depicts inner experiences inspired by fantasy, plots of esoteric literature and existential prose of the 20th century.

In his own words, he has "always tried to shed the burden of culture, which only hinders true, sincere expression in art."

Since 2019, he has been supported by the ANO Outsideville. The works are in the collections of INYE, "Outsideville", as well as in private collections in museums in Germany, England, France.

Psychedelic band and acidether

Since childhood Ilya has been actively interested in sound, discovering the huge and amazing world of experimental music, gathering a musical collection of "weird music", which is getting bigger every day. He studies playing piano, flute, saxophone, and synthesizer.

In 2019 gathers from friends a musical group The Psychedelic Band, and after a year records his first album, periodically performing in small clubs, at exhibitions and themed events. At the moment Psychedelic Band has 8 full-fledged avant-garde-experimental albums.

In parallel with the activities in Psychedelic Band, Ilya develops his solo project acidether, creating surreal worlds in his music, combining incongruous elements of the sound universe, hoping to get some form of life, thus expanding the space of modern avant-garde, pulling dada out of the dark closet of experimental music. Actively working in this direction Ilya creates a whole series of albums, collaborating with different musicians from Russia, Germany, France and Argentina. At the moment acidether has 30 full-length albums. Acidether's music has recently been frequently featured on the airwaves of FM Crisol 92.3 mhz on the program OTHER STIMULOS. Los Polvorines, Argentina

Links :

http://outsider-art.ru/tsaryov

https://www.discogs.com/ru/artist/7960477-Acidether

https://vk.com/id60661092

https://proza.ru/avtor/acidether

Also by Ilya Tsarev

Sueño georgiano
Georgian Dream
Грузинская мечта

About the Publisher

BoyJah Publishing LLC: Amazing and essential content for your eyes and for your brain and for your soul!